POSTHUMOUS EXAMINATIONS

-A POETRY COLLECTION-

JG FEDERMAN

POET PRESS®

SEATTLE · BOTHELL

POET PRESS®

PO BOX 117

Bothell WA, 98041

TITLE DEVISED BY JG FEDERMAN
COVER & INTERIOR DESIGN BY JG FEDERMAN
WRITTEN BY JG FEDERMAN

Cover Image: Courtesy of the Getty's Open Content Program
James Anderson (British, 1813 - 1877), The Dying Gaul (~1845-1855)
Albumen silver print, 28.6 x 41 cm (11 1/4 x 16 1/8 in.)
The J. Paul Getty Museum, Los Angeles.

The Getty Museum did not endorse this project or
participate in its creation.

POET PRESS is a trademark of Poet Press, LLC.

www.poetpress.com

10 9 8 7 6 5 4 3 2 1

First Edition

Printed in the United States of America
Library of Congress Control Number: 2015939054

ISBN-13: 978-1-940158-07-5 (paperback)
ISBN-10: 1940158079 (paperback)
ISBN-13: 978-1-940158-08-2 (ebook)
ISBN-10: 1940158087 (ebook)

For all things bright and red

CONTENTS

CONTENTS

CONTENTS

CONTENTS

CONTENTS

CONTENTS

CONTENTS

ACKNOWLEDGMENTS

I would like to thank my family for their support; their devotion and sacrifices made this book possible. Additionally, those authors and artists who continue to create despite opposition – thank you for being an inspiration.

Morning

"Poetry is eternal. Fashioned by mortals for gods

to enjoy."

— JG Federman

-POEM 1-

POSTHUMOUS EXAMINATIONS

Examine the life which was spent. Like colors dried on pallet knives. Beyond the realm of history's muse, heaven's eyes, and starry heights.

Into oblivion – time has passed.

All things mortal now are cast.

Nihilist thought to plunder the doom.

Black night, burning bright.

O

-POEM 2-

GHASTLY NIGHTS OF SPITE?

Ghastly nights of spite?
Light.
Trembling hours,
cowers.
Glowing homes,
unknown.
Bliss, miss,
prints, scents.

-POEM 3-

GRAFTED EDGE

Grafted edge,
Battered ledge.
Bed, end.
Sleepless eyes,
Needled heights.
Cry, sigh.
Tonight dies.

O

-POEM 4-
REVITALIZE THE NIGHT

Revitalize the night?
Ever on in primal sight.
Hope, floats.
Notes, unknown.
  Fly, high,
Glowing plight.

-POEM 5-

DARKER CORNERS

D arker, corners.
Fog lights.
Beached waves,
Hindsight.
Boredom,
Reflecting.
Suspecting, relenting.
Tick tock, bottoms up.

O

-POEM 6-

RANDOM QUESTION

Random question,
posed inflection.
Illumination, depravation.
Steely horned deception.
Soulful retribution.

-POEM 7-

PITTANCE NOW?

Pittance now?
Glib remark.
    Pish posh,
Autumn's march.
    Green, spring,
April sings.
    Rain, drain.
Lame, brain.

-Poem 8-
Goodbye, cry

Goodbye, cry.
Lies, starlight!
Glass, mass,
Try, alright!

-POEM 9-
WHERE I WALK IS NO CONCERN

Where I walk is no concern,
Tis flittering ghosts of passion's past.
Erupted sense of voided homes.
Hearts and chests of wounded laments.
Where the sea turns grey,
And foamy green.
Turtle doves and ink display.
Christened oceans, born this day.
Engraft the steps of night I take.

O

-POEM 10-

CHASMS LOVE

Chasms love,
    dripping talons shown.
    Cause unknown,
withered gloves.
    Soaring depths,
        cautious breaths.

-POEM 11-

IT WAS IN THE DARK IT CRIED

It was in the dark it cried,
the depths it sighed.
A low groaning moan –
from a soul.
Amidst the burning lake –
where embers quake.
Lava flows,
cool water goes.
Hellish plight.
Frightful sights of
demon wings –
beyond the realm of eternity.

-POEM 12-
DOOM

Gloomy, darkened halls. Piercing grey,
expansive plight. Burning night,
capsized heights.
Hellish purchase, mountainous gripes.
Yelling,
curses far out in sight.
Betwixt satisfaction, callous piety.
Incredulous demons overwhelm thee.
Naught subversity, naked virginity.
Doom, doom, doom, doom.

-POEM 13-
DEAD MAN

Rotting wretch, the dead man lies,
lawful charm lost, victimization gone –
be gone death! (Our wish is nigh).
Kremlin hordes, UN forces. Bloody causes
American forces!
Expressionless the dead man breathes!
Rainy waters of soothing glee,
Pleasant odes of tearing angels.
To shower the earth and flower morn.
Blanketed tufts of flesh are lost.

-Poem 14-

Consider death?

Consider death?
Cast it aside.
Life grants dreams,
fleeting scenes.
Breathless heights,
  and torturous skies.
More to being,
  happiness overrated.

-POEM 15-
GHASTLY SENSE

Ghastly sense,
sweet coalescence.
Stitch, stitch,
pin, pin.
Glassy stare,
dismal care.
Push, pull,
Call, lull.

O

-POEM 16-

WHEN THE WEST CAUGHT FIRE

When the West caught fire,
I was there. Memories shattered,
amidst 9/11's smoky flares.
Murderous hate, flames anew. Inside my mind –
fury still burns more than a decade now.
Forgiveness? No, never.
Tempest keeps guard my heart. Chains of disgust
bar my toleration.
Are the winds of change ever neat? Easy speak,
my words requited.
When the towers toppled, armies battled. The
villains cowered, and cowered long!
Death came swiftly to drag them past Hades'
own tomb. For even the burning chalice of hell
was too good for them.
Their rebellious cause of fanatical fancy –
was granted only by oblivion's halls. As they all
lay silent, cold, and quiet.

-POEM 17-

BELLOWS DEEP

Bellows deep,
Horns unchained.

Death, class.

Social outings flop.

Dates tremble,

Fears resemble.

Fail?

FAIL.

-POEM 18-

ELEGY TO MYSELF

I was that body you see there.
That now lies cold, and lifeless;
Yet defiant in death. Memories rust,
Poems left undone. Where are the fears now?
Like the wounded gunshots echo heights.
I let the sphere of vitality down,
And crossed the face of the starry curves.
Come wanton fury, cringing metal hell.
Dark, dark shifting plates. Burial shrouds.
Beyond the depths of earthy stories,
To the fields below Elysium's glory.
Tripping body – short spirit.
Sifting soul that flitters on.
Shine on love, beat on poetry.
Engraft the hallows with this my prose.

-POEM 19-

DEATHLESS SIGHS, PERILOUS HIGHS

Deathless sighs,

perilous highs.

Dream, dream.

Swimming seas.

O

-POEM 20-

INCREDULITY'S FINEST FIT

Incredulity's finest fit —
The Devil's doors wind the spirit.
Clish, clash.
Eternity passes —
minds falter.

-POEM 21-

INTO THE ABYSS IT WAKES

Into the abyss it wakes,
  The subtle breezes of fiery May.
  Crackled form of age –
be gone the callous waves of change!
Loose these chains of bondage,
Release it from this cage.
For in Hell, death waits to cover thee –
in shrouds of faith and villainous praise.

-Poem 22-

Bungled sinews

Bungled sinews of the mind,
tensions rise like lava highs.
For in deathless desperation the eyes close.
As shutters break the silence of aging days.

-Poem 23-

Death never saw a flower

Death never saw a flower,
For its shadow occluded it.
Death never kissed the sunlight,
For its heart had withered.
Death never felt the rain fall,
For its sadness darkened the day.
Death never witnessed a smile,
For alone in Hell it waits.

O

-POEM 24-

MY JOURNEY

I rested,
but it was not welcomed.
I felt time fade,
but I resisted.
  I wandered,
but was never lost.
  I died,
but never lived.

-POEM 25-

FATE

Actually it was fate which held me,
When those scenes of memories abated.
Flee –
flee!
Summer wind –
From the force of hate and whimsy ends.

-POEM 26-

BENEATH THE GROUND

Beneath the cold, hard ground –
Human hearts lie.
Silent, torn.
Broken, bored.
Even time stayed for a while,
Until fate departed.
Peace entered and woke those hearts.
They followed eagerly.
There were regions of fate to walk in,
Caverns of hate to scare them,
In those fitting plights of earthly shrines.
Peace finally said, *now go and find your way.*

-POEM 27-

PITIFUL PITTANCE

Pitiful pittance –
I doth lie,
Amongst the stars and silvery heights.
Wouldst thou break them,
Or shatter the skies?
For the moons below the celestial divine –
Dive deep into the darkened depths –
Where I cannot go.

-POEM 28-

LIFE FALLS

Life falls, like the rain within a storm,
And shatters like a mirror on cold stone.
Sometimes life flitters about, like
a leaf tumbles.
Other times, it falters –
And spirals out of control.
But sometimes...
Sometimes, life just glides –
Like a seagull in the breeze.
Higher it soars until it is seen no more.

-POEM 29-
CROSSING FATES

Crossing fates collided until the heavens
were gone
The day was done.
Hapless faces poured the dust
Some had never lived.
I saw my face in the desert sun
It was a burden.
I was alone
Why was this my fate?
Had I not cherished faith
Or ruled with iron justice?
Perhaps this was all there was
Sultry death.
Loneliness.

-Poem 30-

Vagrant forms

Vagrant forms took hold of me
I died.
Happiness left me
I tried.
Sadness threw itself upon me
I cried.
Despair gutted me
I screamed.
Love burned me
I fell.

-POEM 31-

BEAUTY BORE ME

Beauty bore me
But I was not her kin.
Love surrounded me
But I was not her type.
Truth empowered me
But I was not her muse.
Death grasped me
And I let her take hold
For only she wanted me.

-POEM 32-

PUNISHMENT

The quiet air punished me
Death swooped in to touch me.
Darkness cried
Tears fried.
The heat crumpled my eyes
My skin crept.
Ghastly sense
Miserable pretext.
Die, die.
Dismal sights.

-POEM 33-

WHEN DEATH TOOK ME

When death took me
sight arrived.
When she released me
I felt alright.
Life left
Peace fled.
Sleep faded
Eternity placated.
Hell bent
Fire crept.
Bliss ignored my advance
And love?
Love fell.

Afternoon

passing thoughts

"The march of prose continues; a song ethereal

a beat immeasurable."

— JG Federman

-POEM 34-

ANGELIC DEMONS

T aken from the steely night
Among dreams of passion and starry nights.
To the underworld
Where fiery lakes await.

Deafening wails and tearing fate

Courage lost and fear remade.

Truth revealed deceit

Revered hopes cried out for mistakes.

Hell burned

Heaven spurned.

Foes fought

Mortals sought.

Gods died

Men died.

Creation died

When angelic demons rose from the mind.

-POEM 35-

VILLAINOUS PLIGHT

Remembrance died in the stench of flesh
The doubtful form of man faded.
Even the heavens closed their gates
For the rot of Hell was long.
In the breathing chasms of the deep
Venom dripped.
Darkness, mist
Dreary essence.
When villainous plight cuts short men's lives.

-POEM 36-

SOUL BREATH

I felt the sweetness fall to the wind,
That last breath sauntered in the sky.
I know the angels saw it –
For my eyes had not yet died.
In the autumn air it waved goodbye,
For the last time I cried.
Funny, though, my soul had never left –
For it never did arrive.

O

-POEM 37-

REACHING GRAVES

Reaching graves caught me
They pulled me under.
Below the earth to a steely tomb,
There, Fate mounted me
Sleep entered me,
Passion filled me.
But death?
Death watched.

-POEM 38-

GLOOMY DOOM

It stood like a vagrant tyrant,
The scowl of dismal ends.
Bloody friends,
Hateful trends.
Gloomy doom awaits –
Hapless tries try.
Boring notes sigh,
Blissful kisses die.
Run, why?
Death cannot die.

-POEM 39-

LOVE'S END

Well, it ended.
Sanctity withdrew from me.
Serenity bled upon my stone face.
Sensuality's tears consumed me.
And love?
Love swooned.

-POEM 40-
THE HALLOWS SHOOK

The hallows shook
For murder stood.
Cold, it stung.
Steely passion.
Bright it bled,
Tears it shed.
The hallows shook,
The end was near.
Fast it ran,
Death it spread.
Dark plight,
Dreary screams.
Wailing walls
And gory scenes.
The hallows shook,
The night I died.

-POEM 41-
THE GOLDEN GARDEN

What darkened the golden garden?

Fate.

Did peace lose its light?

No.

Death came, spirits waved.

Hate. Hate.

Splayed day.

(silence)

(silence)

fade away.

-Poem 42-

My Memoir

I looked for you
and wrote:
My muse you found me

I rested and you spoke:
Rescue me

I fell upon my pen
To save the life we built.

Now muse, I must depart:
To meet you in heaven's hills.
And run inside your mind.

O

-POEM 43-

STEELY CLUBS

I crafted those steely clubs,
When the beating forms of night cried out.
(wails)

Bliss echoed screams.

I sighed.

The beatings ceased.

Breathe,

Slowly.

Bleeding beams.

(dripping)

-POEM 44-

LINE OF SIGHT

Justice found a home in highest heaven,
But anger stayed below.
Hope made a brilliant star,
While jealousy rocked the waters of the damned.
All this was seen from another world away,
Upon a mountain, topped with grey.

-POEM 45-

TERROR

Jaws cleft,
Burned meat.
(Fangs snap)
Why me?
Nightmares crumpled,
The earth turned to dust.
Fire consumed the heavens,
Ice froze its hold.
I shattered my heart,
And fell alone into bliss.

-POEM 46-

NIGHTMARE

It sat.
(quietly)
I watched.
(silently)
Suddenly –
(horror)
Frightened fears plundered my heart.
(pain)
Nihilist thoughts overpowered me.
(terror)
I woke –
it was a dream.
(sigh)
I was still alive.

-POEM 47-

TREK OF PLIGHT

The celestial orbs rose,
And travelled faster around the sky.
(whoosh)
Far into the night.
But I carried them –
their weight alone was mine.
They fell upon me,
I cried.
But I threw their lights into the vast expanse –
So that they could illuminate the universe
for everyone to see.

-POEM 48-
WHEN THE UNIVERSE ENDED

The earth shook,
(rumble)
Oceans quaked.
(thunder)
Feelings dissipated,
My soul ruptured.
When the universe ended –
My breath ceased.
The heavens fell upon the ground,
The stars ignited me –
I burned and burned.
I woke, not in death, but steely mist.
Cool, grey eyes greeted me,
Eucalyptus buried me.

-POEM 49-

LIFE SAID

Burned mist consumed me that spring,
The summer winds had changed me.
The winter ice plagued me,
And the autumn colors crushed me.
Trees fell
(crash)
Life bled
(drip)
Pain fled
(thump)
Life said:
Go, if you wish it so.

-POEM 50-

DECEIVING PAIN

Pain, thou art no sting.
Only a close friend.
For friends sting,
Even kill.
They threatened me –
Their voices maimed.
Callous words of hate and anger.
Deceive them all,
Let them wander:
The hills of eternity –
Alone forever.

-POEM 51-

LAKE OF FIRE

The fires of the deep poured forth,
Into a great lake which stretched
before me.
A cool water flowed nearby,
In this dream.
But soon it was consumed by torture,
The fire burned it bright.
Yet the water endured –
Its fate was not forged.
In misty vapor –
It stood forever.
Like eternity –
Running on and on,
And on.

-POEM 52-

DEATH'S SPAWN

In death it spawned
   (wait)
The steely life of fate
(break)
Howling nights of dawn
(roar)
Bleeding heights of homes
(door creaks)
Blithering blossoms fainted
(wind chimes)
Time froze
(crickets)
When death's spawn of hate arose
(maniacal laughter)
In the glistening arms of the red, red rose

O

-POEM 53-

HELLSCAPE

Death spoils
Falter.
Winds captive

Horror.

Blade frighten

Tighten.

Snow whitens.

Poorer.

-POEM 54-

HELL SPIRIT

Nearer, clearer
Hidden fears.
Thrashing, gnashing
Bitten ears.

Grasp, claw

Fight, fly

Into burning chasms of the night.

O

-Poem 55-

Assaulted sense

Assaulted sense
Bridled ease.
Death awaits
Marked by thee.

Hell.

Fire.

(burning)

(choking)

Falling

Falling

falling

f
a
l
l
i
n
g

-POEM 56-

AGONY AWAITS

Agony awaits –
I saw it in a dream.
Fleeting forms,
Spectre hordes.
Enveloped sense,
Bridled breaths.
Death, death
Burning death.
Red cuts,
Heartfelt
Chest pounds,
Sweat sounds.
Breath, breath,
Fleeting breath.
Chasms, fire,
Gloomy sense.

O

-POEM 57-

PURCHASE HILLS

I purchased hills long ago
To mark my grave –
But no one came to clear the wood.
I waited, while the autumn leaves faded.
Like the dying colors whispered –
I too died.
Waiting for the world to catch up –
No one, nothing –
Could see that coming.
Not even me.

-Poem 58-

Icy gleams

Icy gleams flitter about
Like torrents they scatter.
Piercing, cutting they tear the soul.
Wavering it falters,
Tumbling it falls.
Crystal eyes deceive,
Floating whims die.
Soulless essence pries.
Fly, fly into the night.

-POEM 59-

BLACKENED SENSE

I heard it said in hell:
All sense burns. To ash it becomes.
Blackened presence, dreary coalescence.
Orange flames,
Heated brains.
Drums in the fire,
Windy spires.
Tame spears,
Flint nears.
(stab)
Torture –
Stake.

-POEM 60-

POWER

Power was never for the weak to wield
I saw it in the ashen fields.
Quietly it waited
Silently it prayed.
Bitter ends for sweet days
Cold breaths splayed.
Ink bled
Time shattered.
Life dripped vicariously away.

-POEM 61-

BOUND

Blessings fell from heaven
But the damned could not find them.
For their silver wings were clouded
By the darkened night of hell.
Love fell from the stars
But the demons ate them.
For their taste was divine
Like the golden apples of paradise.
I reached for the stars
But was consumed by fire.
I caught love but it broke my heart.
The demons laughed
Their smoky eyes cried.
Lucifer stayed their jokes
And bound my life to hell.

-POEM 62-

PLUMMETING BREATHS

Plummeting breaths
I rise
Cloven hills

I climb

Broken wings

I fly

Tortured soul

I die

Bitterness

I fight

Loneliness

I cry

O

-POEM 63-

SPECIAL MORALS

Why impose special limits to morals?
Does it rob them of a
meaningful significance?
Are they not devalued then?
Cast aside the boundaries which confine,
Let loose the furies' fate.
Conceived morality –
Blood still flows.
To the gloomy depths
And pits thou knows.

-POEM 64-

COSMIC STRIFE

I cowered in the cold, icy realm of heaven
That region forsaken by the gods
Where the expanse of cosmic dust advanced
the doom of night
Alone I trembled and shook
The blithering winds bellowed
Around me the cosmos clustered
Choking life to death.

-POEM 65-

BRIMSTONE BODIES

Brimstone bodies gather
In the horrid night they strike.
Shuffled sounds of chains
Ignite the plight they face.
Lo! The moon quakes
The earth begins to crumble.
For out of the depths demons rise
To purge the planet one more time.

-POEM 66-
BONDAGE FORMS

Doubtful, dubious forms awake
The threatening eyes of Lucifer's gleam
Piercing, deceiving.
Lying, cheating.
Demonic hate and retribution
Domination and simple infusion.
Divine castration –
Lowly states.
Poor, poor souls
Bondage estate.

NIGHT

TWILIGHT'S HOUR

"THE SILENCE IS BROKEN WITH PARODIES OF PROSE."

— JG FEDERMAN

-POEM 67-

SHATTERED HEAVEN

Torrents of Elysium
Falling, tumbling down.
Flittered sense of belonging –
Troubled breaths of suffering.
Sleep, sleep.
Deep, deep.
Shattered hopes are fading
Bloody swords engulfing.
The haven of homes is ending
Doom, doom.
(crash)

-POEM 68-
HELL'S EPOCH

Fabricated epochs of the time
Eons pass, yet love is sublime.
Divine even, it has been said
A feeling which humanity bred.
For to flee the time and rising tides
All will be lost and cast aside.
In the deep, dark doom of steely jaws
The promise of life in love's awes.

-POEM 69-

BEYOND LIFE

For into death I will follow thee,
Nay, further still.
To the deep, dark bowels of hell.
I will wage war for thee
Yet no one can find their way alone.
Tis thy heart to guide me love
Or shall I walk beside thee?
Instill that passion so that I may find
Thy soul in the next life –
The life sublime.

O

-Poem 70-
Thou called

I could not hear thee when thou called
For the rhythms of life had captured me.
Yes, I succumbed my love to those gasping breaths
In dreamy thoughts of golden threads.
That the sun breaths out upon the earth
In its gentle shower of raging power.
But thou didst call again and I didst answer
As the sunrise cleft, moonbeams leapt
And danced on the water in its silvery pool
To ask the angels for starry beds.

-POEM 71-

SCORCHED EARTH

Scorched earth –
most foul
Relent!
The gnashing teeth of brimstone fires awake
The door was opened:
Doom, doom.
The horde of Hell released.

-Poem 72-

Righteous guise

I saw the empty shells of life before me –
Oh horrid curse of immortality!
It consumed me.
And now, the righteous guise falls
Into red, red pools of sultry plight.

-POEM 73-
CELL

For there were several sad verses of death
In that list of plagued night.
The book was read, the chains unlocked
My cell was turned about.
Released into stony cages
Beckoned sense relieving
Feeling:
Trapped.
(door locks)

O

-POEM 74-

DECAYING FLESH

Its putrid stench consumed me
I fell.
And the whispered sense of decaying flesh
wafted throughout the cavern
Then the beasts came.
They tore at my limbs and dismembered my core
I cried.
Death raised its sickle
And I died.

-POEM 75-

REST

With the world of rest I bled
In the night I felt dreary dread.
Resting blood.
Stagnant faith.
Falling dreams.

-POEM 76-

WHEN THE NIGHT RISES

Brevity's night arises
The consuming flames of goddess Isis
Hells bells
Red devils
Falling demons
Blissful heathens

-POEM 77-

THE ONTOLOGICAL LEAP YEAR BOOK

I read that book:
The ontological leap year.
Afterward I asked:
Where does the voice of altruism come from?
Goodness had no reply
Death sighed
Joy cried.
Peace asked:
What do you wish for?
And I replied:
My wife

-POEM 78-

MAN'S PHILOSOPHY

Every man should have written his
account of philosophy.
For the winds of change pervade them.
The wars of the earth consume them.
And the fate of death confuses them.

-Poem 79-

Three fates

There were three fates –
All of which I grew to hate
Dreary faces
Sunken eyes
Alluring voices
But most of all, their
Dismal cries

-POEM 80-

WHEN THE MOON DIED

The night the moon died
Hell froze.
The flames ceased
But the torrent raged.
The earth tilted
And life faltered.
The oceans ceased their tumble
And the silence melted the singing stars.

-POEM 81-

FLEETING FORMS

I stood apart and stared –
At those silent, fleeting forms.
They broke my bones
And shattered my mind.
The sleepy essence of death caressed me
Longingly it tormented my spirit.
Then ripped my heart to shreds.

-Poem 82-

Age

C left age
War created
Life faded
Love abated
Death pervaded

-POEM 83-

DEEP

Faces in the deep
Gloomy deep.
Cries in the night
Black night.
Horrors in hell
Red Hell.
Death in dreams
Dreary dreams.

-POEM 84-

THE FALL

I fell deeper my love into that pit
A chasm roaring with fire.
But the fire didst not pierce me,
Nor burn my flesh,
Twas a fire of torrential love and furious passion.
Its entwined sense of intimacy overpowered me
And I fell into the lake of the sublime –
Alone.
And I sank, deeper into that mire
Where love's lost dwell.
And I didst not find thee there
So I swam beyond the lake into a great sea
Yet the waves crashed down upon me.
Their lapping kisses consumed me
And as I floundered in the great ocean
A ship came by.

The ship was thee – for it bore thy own name
And I travelled toward thee –
Toward the great expanse of the sea
Where the horizon cleft the sun from its lofty throne.
But I didst not find thee beyond the horizon
So I travelled further toward the looming expanse
Where silver threads dangled
From a starry heaven above
And a dewy essence pervaded each crystal
So I climbed and climbed further.
Twas there I saw thee –
Garbed in starlight.
White robes love, akin to the moon's kind
And from that height I surveyed the earth
And all outstretched before it.
I closed my eyes and dreamed of thee
As thou held me tightly amongst the cosmic seams –
And I slept dear love
A peaceful sleep
Never to wake or falter
For I became lost in thy shade
And eternal ways.

-POEM 85-

TEMPTING FATES

As I bravely tempted fate
The world prayed.
My chains abated
But the demons waited.

-POEM 86-

STEELY SILENCE

At once I woke in hell
The red screams pervaded me
From long lost souls.
And the bones of the rhythms were marred
In the steely silence of their jaws.

-POEM 87-

TASSELS OF TIME

The tassels of time unwound as I fell
Deeper into the pits of anguish
There I languished, toiled, and bled
Amidst the fleeting form of life I led.
My spirit watched and wept
For I could no longer cry:
The ashen plight of hell had robbed me of my tears.

-POEM 88-
FADING

Your face –
It danced in the dark.
Pools –
They fell in the stars.
Blossoms –
Burned the pale blue skies.
Fire –
Ignited my soul.

-POEM 89-

FIGHT FEAR

To fight the face of fear
Night is thy name.
To purge the earth of hate
Death thou art near.
March on doom to that lively end
Beyond the dark and starry beds.
Lay in the tranquil, vital wakes
Where the ink of space resounds.
The brilliant reign of heavenly hosts
Utter against foes and demon ghosts.

-POEM 90-

FATIGUE

Fatigued I fly –
Into the wily night.
What hope is left for me?
The hope of dreamy dreams.

-POEM 91-

ELYSIUM

Heaven is but a whimsy place
I saw it from a lofty height.
The stars showed me its gates
The mouth of Hell opened its face.

-POEM 92-

WILT

As a rose doth wilt,
   So doth I for thee oh Muse!
   Thou gave me more than song and rhyme:
I found the bleeding heart of time.
Age, Muse thou knows her name
No secret to conceal.
For her arms wrap tightly around me
And pull me down to earth.
Below the dusty dirt
Beneath the sands of sight.
(sinking feeling)
(dreaming)
(gasping)
(silence)

-POEM 93-

SOUL'S LIFE

Yet I saw it once before –
Gasping for its own breath.
The soul's life:
Its own republic to structure itself.
Upon news it fell –
like war and peace.
The fainting days of sunlight rays.
To gleam a part of blooming sense
As leaves doth fall to autumn's breast.

-POEM 94-

LIFE'S GIFT

Peace spoke.
Death quaked at her voice
It could not look her in the eye.
Love spoke.
Death swooned at her kiss
It could not resist her embrace.
But I did not tremble at the voice of peace
Or fall prey to love's lips.
For life granted me both things –
To enjoy a time of bliss.

-POEM 95-

DEMON DEATH

In dubious fashion the lives of demons were lost
The grasping fate of Hell brought death
upon itself.
Fire consumed them
Eternity devoured their souls.
Mortal man bellowed and the heavens faltered
And the Devil cursed the earth
But it swallowed him whole.

-POEM 96-

FIERY FEELINGS

Feelings –
    They fell
      Broken like shards of glass.
I saw the onrush of red death await the damned
Their torment stirred the sea of doom.
The burning plight of Hell's fumes consumed me
I collapsed and fainted.
Death hovered above me
And his hand touched mine.
I died:
not once, but twice.
Passion and beauty fell –
They fell like shards of ice.

-POEM 97-

VENTURED NIGHT

In the steely ventures of the night
the demons rhymed.
Their master devised
The soul was chastised.
Hate beat and rage seethed
Yet the glimmering fangs of death still bleed.

-POEM 98-

STARRY STEPS

Steps to vanquish the days
That is what the stars were.
Their tumultuous shimmering curtailed
the heavens
Blinded the eyes of gods.
Even I could not reach them
But I tried.
They burned me up
In brilliant light.

O

-POEM 99-

COLORS OF DEATH

D eath's colors bled
Black.
The red, red landscape faded.

(zoom out)

Death could not relax

(sigh)

The earth groaned.

Even the cosmos turned.

(grinding)

But death,

Death was still there.

-POEM 100-

THE FATE OF BLISS

Death swallowed bliss
And tossed it to the stars.
Their hollowed shells were shattered –
Those remnants of the gods.
Bliss kissed them
But they were lifeless.
It careened off into the distance
Fate faded.
Slowly
Wasted.

O
-POEM 101-
TO THE MEMORY OF LIFE: AN ELEGY

When all time and loves hath passed,
The music stops her advance.
In her stately garb and starlit hair,
Lives are lost and planets left bare.

For all breath dost stop and lie in flame; [5]
Among darkened corners and cavernous ways.
Who thinks that souls will last the day,
And span the hills of dewy May?
Where life hast gone, its relic still;

Lost in fathoms deep and trenches filled. [10]
Forever eternal struggles cleft,
Loves from Earth and its starry depths.
So carry that torch of impending doom;
For those that seek her fateful tomb,

Shall wake in marveled day. [15]
For the eyes of nature live to see,
A busy bed of rosy threads.
Like burning ships in the skies of heaven,
The cosmic score hath struck eleven.

Beyond shoals of diamond tears and whimsy coves,[20]
With single notes and poems of hope.
For who can say that life was naught,
When love alone is held aloft?

Index of Titles

About the Author

JG Federman is an award–winning educator and poet. He is the author of *The Muses: Epic Odes*, *Art: Quotations of Inspiration*, and *Leadership Quotations for Success*. Mr. Federman has been published in scholarly journals for his academic work and writes the "Featured Plant" article for a local botanical garden. He has several forthcoming titles to be published by Poet Press.

POSTHUMOUS
EXAMINATIONS

POET PRESS®

WWW.POETPRESS.COM

PO BOX 117 · BOTHELL · WA · 98041

www.ingramcontent.com/pod-product-compliance
Lightning Source LLC
Chambersburg PA
CBHW021159020426
42331CB00003B/134